Barnegat Lighthouse

PERSPECTIVES

David Biggy

Schiffer Publishing Ltd®
4880 Lower Valley Road, Atglen, PA 19310

DEDICATION

Dedicated to Melissa, because it all started here.

Library of Congress Control Number: 2009942241

Designed by John P. Cheek
Cover design by Bruce Waters
Type set in Humanist 521 BT

ISBN: 978-0-7643-3454-2
Printed in China

Published by Schiffer Publishing Ltd.
4880 Lower Valley Road
Atglen, PA 19310
Phone: (610) 593-1777; Fax: (610) 593-2002
E-mail: Info@schifferbooks.com

ACKNOWLEDGMENTS

First, many thanks to the Schiffer Publishing team for another wonderful opportunity to share my photography with Barnegat Lighthouse fans across the world. Second, thanks to Diane Coppola-Fritz and Elaine Coppola at Island Arts in Ship Bottom, N.J., for the use of some great historical photos of Old Barney, which add nostalgia I otherwise wouldn't have been able to include here. Finally, thanks to all those who enjoy my work and make it a part of their homes and offices.

INTRODUCTION

Trouble was brewing for Barnegat Lighthouse in 1855.

A new light tower had to be constructed at the site, because the one standing there at the time was threatened by erosion along Barnegat Inlet. Lieutenant George G. Meade was brought in by the U.S. Lighthouse Board to fix the problem, and Meade was intent on making the new tower built to last.

The first light tower built at Barnegat Inlet, using a congressional appropriation of $6,000, was a 40-foot masonry tower constructed by Winslow Lewis, a retired sea captain. It stood about 900 feet from the ocean. The original tower was put into service in July 1835, and by 1845 only 450 feet remained between the tower and the ocean.

After construction began on the present tower in 1856, the light was removed from the original tower in 1857 and temporarily housed in a wooden tower further inland, where it stayed until the new tower was completed. During construction of the present tower, the original lighthouse and keeper's cottage were destroyed and washed away by the sea.

After the first tower was washed away by the waters of Barnegat Inlet in 1857, the current Barnegat Lighthouse was erected in 1858 and put into service on Jan. 1, 1859. Courtesy of Island Arts/used with permission

When Meade drew up the plans for the current tower that is Barnegat Lighthouse, which stands 100 feet south of where the original tower was washed away, it is difficult to know whether he figured his creation would still be standing even fifty years later. After all, the currents within what Dutch explorer Cornelius May dubbed "Barendegat," or "Breakers Inlet," in 1614 generated fierce conditions during big storms. Erosion was a huge threat to anything standing within several hundred feet of the inlet.

About 30 years after the current Barnegat Lighthouse was first lighted, in 1889, a twenty-room triplex dwelling was constructed to house the keepers and his two assistants who tended to the lighthouse and surrounding grounds, creating an impressive site for those unfamiliar with the territory. Courtesy of Island Arts/used with permission

Meade was one of the U.S. Army Bureau of Topographical Engineers' best structural designers. His job was to come up with a light tower that would not only stand against winter nor'easters and summer hurricanes, but hold its place among the shifting sands of "Breakers Inlet."

Based closely on the plans he had drawn up for Absecon Lighthouse, which was first put into service in 1857 some 40 miles south of Barnegat Inlet, Meade designed another structural marvel. His recommendation for a "first-class light" was built under the watchful eye of construction supervisor Lt. W.S. Reynolds.

In 1889, a twenty-room, two-story triplex was built to house the keeper and his two assistants assigned to tend to the light and grounds, but in 1920, after several winter storms caused further erosion, the structure was sold to salvagers and razed within a few weeks.

The fact that Old Barney has stood for more than 150 years is a testament to its construction — with some 675 thousand bricks, an outer wall with a thickness of four and a half feet at the base, and an inner cylindrical wall nine inches thick throughout the tower's 163 feet. The inlet had shifted hundreds of feet southward since Cornelius May and his band of explorers first embarked on the area, and the constant threat of erosion always remained.

Despite all the threats, Meade's creation, often referred to by locals as Old Barney, stood strong for many years as a crucial marker for mariners sailing west from Europe along the 40th Parallel. In fact, Old Barney was the turning point toward New York for sixty-eight years.

A year after the lighthouse was turned over to the State of New Jersey in 1926, Barnegat Lighthouse was decommissioned and replaced by Barnegat Lightship, stationed eight miles offshore. The first-order Fresnel lens, designed and made by Henri LePaute in Paris, France, was then removed from the lantern room and sent to Staten Island for safekeeping. The lighting fixture was six feet in diameter, ten feet high, and formed from more than 1,000 separate glass prisms and twenty-four bull's-eye lenses mounted to a brass frame weighing nearly five tons.

Prior to being completely discontinued as a navigational aid in 1944, several efforts to save the lighthouse were made, including one in the early 1930s which included the development of an emergency jetty created from old trucks, cars, and baby carriages. In 1934, the federal government appropriated $12,000 to reinforce the grounds surrounding the lighthouse in an effort to cut down on the erosion near the base of the tower, which at that point stood just two feet from the water at high tide.

Since the mid-1920s, when the Department of Congress refused to fund any further projects at the lighthouse, many painstaking efforts have taken place in order to keep the current tower from suffering the same fate as the previous tower.

Fortunately, since the grounds surrounding the lighthouse were designated a state park in 1957 — 100 years after construction began on the tower — permanent jetties were set in place to the north at the south end of Island Beach State Park and to the south of the lighthouse, and they seemed to have helped cut down on the erosion near the tower.

During a $660,000 project starting in 1988 and ending in 1991, the lighthouse underwent renovations to its masonry, brick, and stone portions, as well as the cast-iron section of the lantern and gallery. After reopening to the public in June 1991, Old Barney went another thirteen years before being temporarily closed for a new paint job, which revitalized its red-and-white daymark, the lighthouse's distinct colorization and pattern that mariners of old used as their navigational landmark during daylight hours.

In 2008, the non-profit Friends of Barnegat Lighthouse State Park announced plans to relight the lantern for Old Barney's 150th birthday on January 1, 2009. While the Long Beach Township Fraternal Order of Police Lodge 5 donated $15,000 to acquire a new lamp — ironically the same price tag for the original first-order Fresnel lens back in 1856 — additional funds were raised by the Friends organization to replace the lantern room's windows.

The new lens, imported from Vega Industries in New Zealand, is about 20 inches high and 20 inches wide, made of Lucite panels. A rotating turntable behind the panels sends four beams of light to all points of the compass to deliver a white flash once every ten seconds. The ten-second flash is Old Barney's distinguishing characteristic among the other six lighthouses along New Jersey's Atlantic coast, specifically Absecon, the next lighthouse to the south, and Sea Girt, the next one to the north.

The new light is visible up to 20 nautical miles, and when it was activated for the first time just after 5 p.m. on New Year's Day 2009 I was among thousands who witnessed the historic relighting.

Today, the new-look Barnegat Lighthouse is celebrated not only as a piece of maritime history, but also a testament to the man who designed a structure created to provide hope, comfort, and a welcomed sight to mariners from all over the world, as well as a symbol of strength and durability at the height of the storm.

And it is that historical significance that is celebrated, photographically, throughout this book. During its 150th year in existence, my mission was to take as many photographs of this coastal friend from as many angles as possible, and deliver to all Barnegat Lighthouse enthusiasts a photographic reminder of why we love Old Barney, and why we need to keep its light shining for another 150 years.

After the keeper's house was damaged by storms and subsequently razed in 1920, the encroaching inlet waters caused such terrible erosion that Barnegat Lighthouse eventually had to be surrounded by jetties and required foundation work to solidify the grounds surrounding its base. Courtesy of Island Arts/used with permission

BARNEGAT LIGHTHOUSE KEEPERS

In the days when lighthouses required keepers, before electronic automation took over during the 1900s, it was necessary that each keeper climbed to the lantern room each day to clean and maintain the lanterns and reflectors, light the lamp, trim the wicks every four hours, replenish the oil, wind the clockworks that turned the lamp, and make sure the light was burning brightly throughout the night.

Beginning around the turn of the 19th century, the president appointed keepers to their posts. But in 1952, that duty was turned over to the United States Lighthouse Board, and keepers underwent a three-month probationary period before their full appointment was issued by the Secretary of Treasury. At any time during their service, keepers could be transferred between stations and districts.

After the development of the United States Lighthouse Service in 1910, some lighthouses, including Barnegat Lighthouse, were decommissioned, though their lanterns remained lighted until automation replaced the need for oil lamps. In those instances, keepers were no longer used and the lighthouses were tended on a part-time basis by local citizens called lamplighters and lamp attendants.

During its keeper days, Barnegat Lighthouse had twenty official keepers and two lamplighters. They were:

Henry V. Low (1835-1838, died March 12, 1838)
John H. Low (1838-1839, Henry Low's son)
Ellen S. Low (1839, served one quarter)
Garrett H. Herring (1839-1841, removed June 15, 1841)
Jeremiah Spragg (1841-1846, removed March 12, 1846)
John Allen (1846-1849, removed Nov. 13, 1849)
John Warren (1849-1851)
Charles Collins (1851-1853)
Joseph H. Townsend (1853-1854)
James Fuller (1854-1861, transitioned from first lighthouse to temporary wooden tower, then to current lighthouse)
Hiram M. Horner (1861-1862)
A.B. Brown (1862-1866)
John Kelley (1866-1873, removed Oct. 22, 1873)
William C. Yates (1873-1875, transferred Oct. 9, 1875)
Joshua H. Reeves (1875-1885, transferred Oct. 20, 1885)
Thomas Bills (1885-1896, transferred Oct. 1, 1896)
Abraham G. Wolf (1896, appointment cancelled Dec. 2, 1896)
W.T. Woodmansee (1896-1915)
Clarence H. Cranmer (1915-1926)
Andrew E. Applegate (1926-1928, last official keeper)
Robert E. Applegate (1928-1932, lamplighter)
William E. Rothas (1932-1940, lamplighter)

BARNEGAT LIGHTHOUSE FAST FACTS

First Barnegat Lighthouse tower built: 1834
Height of first tower: 40 feet
Current lighthouse first lighted: January 1, 1859
Number of stairs inside Barnegat Lighthouse: 217
Current tower height: 163 feet
Focal plane of current tower: 175 feet
Number of bricks that make up Barnegat Lighthouse: About 675,000
Original lens: First-order Fresnel lens
Characteristic: One white flash every ten seconds
Daymark: Red upper half, white lower half
GPS Coordinates: 39° 45' 46.91" N - 74° 06' 22.86" W (approximately one mile south of the 40th Parallel)
Diameter at base: 28 feet

In 1957, the grounds surrounding Barnegat Lighthouse became a state park, visited by hundreds of thousands of visitors each year.

On New Year's Day 2009, Barnegat Lighthouse was re-lighted as a navigational aid for the first time since it was decommissioned in 1927.

At 163 feet, Barnegat Lighthouse easily stands out.

Reflections of Barnegat Lighthouse in the inlet waters are frequent, especially when it's a calm day.

Winter time is a great time to visit the state park.

With its new lantern, finding beams of light on foggy nights are a spectacular sight.

With its bright, red-and-white daymark, Barnegat Lighthouse still is easily spotted from any vantage point. Here it is seen from the boardwalk behind Andy's Bait & Tackle.

On some mornings, the view of Barnegat Lighthouse is simply stunning.

Views of Old Barney from across the inlet at Island Beach State Park.

Reflections of Barnegat Lighthouse can come in many forms, day or night.

Visitors to Long Beach Island often bicycle to the state park grounds, even on dreary days.

The scenic nature trail within the park offers great views of Barnegat Lighthouse.

In Barnegat Light, the two tallest structures are Barnegat Lighthouse and the water tower used as an elevated storage container made to hold a water supply at a height sufficient to pressurize the local water distribution system as well as for firefighting purposes. Barnegat Lighthouse is 163 feet tall, while the water tower is 130 feet.

A fiery summer sunset behind the lighthouse.

The moon rises east of Barnegat Lighthouse.

Snow dusts the north end of Long Beach Island.

There are no shortage of vantage points for those seeking them.

Boat traffic is brisk in the inlet, especially as summer approaches.

Sunrises over the Atlantic Ocean provide an awesome view from the inlet side of the lighthouse.

Old Barney turned 150 years old on January 1, 2009, when its new light shone for the first time as nightfall arrived.

With very few visitors in the winter, Barnegat Lighthouse State Park can be a calm, refreshing place to spend an afternoon just walking around and taking in the views.

At one time, Barnegat Lighthouse was lighted by a first-order Fresnel lens.

Whether it's just before sunset or from the tidal pools dotting the rocks along the inlet, Old Barney is a charismatic figure of strength.

As night approaches, fishing boats from nearby Viking Village motor past Barnegat Lighthouse on the way back to port.

Barnegat Lighthouse's new lantern was developed by Vega Industries and imported from New Zealand. It is visible up to twenty nautical miles.

Sometimes, the conditions are just right for a picturesque view of Barnegat Lighthouse.

Blustery conditions at Barnegat Lighthouse often mean some biting winds and even a few snowflakes.

When the sunset is a golden one, Barnegat Lighthouse's signature red-and-white daymark is replaced by a shadowy tower.

No matter what time of year it is, Barnegat Lighthouse State Park is a great place for a morning walk.

For the most part, Barnegat Lighthouse State Park is a desolate place in the winter.

As dusk approached on New Year's Day 2009, the sunset shortly before the re-lighting ceremony provided a great setting for the historic moment.

Once the sun went down on Jan. 1, 2009, the new-look Barnegat Lighthouse was introduced in grand fashion.

Even amid the bare trees of winter, Barnegat Lighthouse is a magnificent sight.

At all times of year, Barnegat Lighthouse remains an attractive structure.

Over the years, Barnegat Lighthouse has become a welcomed sight to boaters and personal watercraft riders alike.

For years, the decorative floodlights offered the only light from the base of the lighthouse, but now Old Barney's new lantern makes its mark in the night sky as well.

A winter sunset casts a nice, warm glow on Barnegat Lighthouse.

For visitors making the trek on the nature trail near the lighthouse, Old Barney almost always commands the center of attention.

Some of the native conifers have been part of the Barnegat inlet landscape for as long as Old Barney has been standing.

If you want to see Barnegat Lighthouse amid the many contrasting perspectives surrounding it, visit the state park in January and February.

Whether the angle is from the southeast (facing page), the west (left), or the northeast (below), the towering, 163-foot tower is a majestic sight.

Before the sun comes up, many fishing boats head out to the Atlantic Ocean via Barnegat Inlet, as Old Barney lights the way.

It's always interesting to see how much Old Barney's red top changes shade and tint with varying conditions and from varying distances.

While most folks visit Barnegat Lighthouse State Park during the warmer months, the colder months offer some wonderful looks at the old lighthouse.

With all the trees to the south of it, you sometimes have to peer through the foliage to see Barnegat Lighthouse.

The middle of the spring is generally a peaceful time at Barnegat Inlet.

As sunset leads to darkness, Barnegat Inlet sometimes becomes a picture of beauty, and at the heart of that landscape is Old Barney.

The jetty leading southward away from Barnegat Lighthouse allows the thousands of folks who visit every year a place to relax and enjoy the sounds and feel of the ocean.

Old Barney, as seen across the inlet from High Bar Harbor.

Before it was decommissioned in 1927, the current Barnegat Lighthouse had eleven different light keepers, starting with James Fuller and ending with Andrew Applegate.

Hordes of people flock to the lighthouse to climb Old Barney.

Every summer, hundreds and sometimes thousands of visitors jam the beach and jetty to the southeast of Barnegat Lighthouse.

Whenever a sunset engulfs Barnegat Lighthouse, it marks another day in the long life of George Meade's creation.

Up close or from afar, Meade's second of three similar lighthouses stands out as something to see.

From just about every part of the state park's southern grounds, you can get a glimpse of Barnegat Lighthouse between the stems of various foliage.

A look into the lantern room is the reward for climbing the 217 stairs to the top.

From inside the 163-foot tower, it's easy to see why Old Barney has stood since its completion in 1858.

During a sunny summer afternoon, Old Barney casts a large shadow on the grounds below. It also casts a great reflection in the nearby cove just outside its western wall (facing page).

In addition to the majestic tower, Barnegat Lighthouse State Park offers plenty of scenery for its visitors.

On a clear day, the views of Barnegat Lighthouse from the inlet side are always lovely.

20

ABOUT THE AUTHOR

David Biggy is a professional sports journalist, writer, and photographer who has lived in Barnegat, N.J., with his wife, Melissa, and stepson, Herb, since 1999. Growing up in North Jersey, David's passion for photography developed during his teen years and grew along with his interest in journalism and writing during his years at Ramapo College of New Jersey. After David and Melissa moved to the Jersey Shore, David's first experience photographing a lighthouse occurred when they visited Barnegat Lighthouse in April 2000.

Photographer David Biggy. Photo by Melissa Biggy.

His lighthouse, sunset, seascape, landscape, and wildlife prints hang in homes and offices in just about every state within the United States and as far away as Russia, proving that folks from all walks of life have an affinity for what his eye sees and his camera captures.

He has photographed about 200 lighthouses and lightships along the East and Gulf coasts and the Great Lakes, and he is a member of several lighthouse organizations, including the New Jersey Lighthouse Society and the American Lighthouse Foundation.

David has had a permanent position at Studio 8 @ Island Arts in Ship Bottom, N.J, since 2008, and you can see more of his work by visiting www.biggysphotosetc.com. David's first book, *Lighthouses: Maine to Florida*, was published in 2009 with Schiffer Publishing, Ltd.